Watery Worlds

CORAL REEFS

Jinny Johnson

W
FRANKLIN WATTS

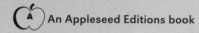 An Appleseed Editions book

Paperback edition 2015

First published in 2011 by Franklin Watts
338 Euston Road, London NW1 3BH

Franklin Watts Australia
Hachette Children's Books
Level 17/207 Kent St, Sydney, NSW 2000

© 2011 Appleseed Editions

Created by Appleseed Editions Ltd,
Well House, Friars Hill, Guestling,
East Sussex TN35 4ET

Designed by Hel James
Edited by Mary-Jane Wilkins
Picture research by Su Alexander
Artwork by Graham Rosewarne

ISBN 978 1 4451 3823 7
Dewey Classification 577.7'89

A CIP catalogue for this book is available from the British Library.

Picture credits
page 7 WILTSHREYEOMAN/Shutterstock; 14 OSF/Photolibrary; 15t Waterborn/Shutterstock;
19b Luiz A Rocha/Shutterstock; 20 Willyam Bradberry/Shutterstock; 21t Wayne Johnson/
Shutterstock, b Liquid Productions LLC/Shutterstock; 22 Pete Niesen/Shutterstock;
23t Nick Poling/Shutterstock, b James van den Broek/Shutterstock; 25t Richard Williamson/
Shutterstock; 26 WaterFrame-Underwater Images/Photolibrary; 27t OSF/Photolibrary,
b Peter Arnold Images/Photolibrary; 29 Stuart Forster/Alamy
All other images from Thinkstock
Front cover main image Thinkstock, below left to right: Thinkstock, Willyam/Shutterstock,
Thinkstock

Printed in China

Franklin Watts is a division of Hachette Children¹s Books,
an Hachette UK company.
www.hachette.co.uk

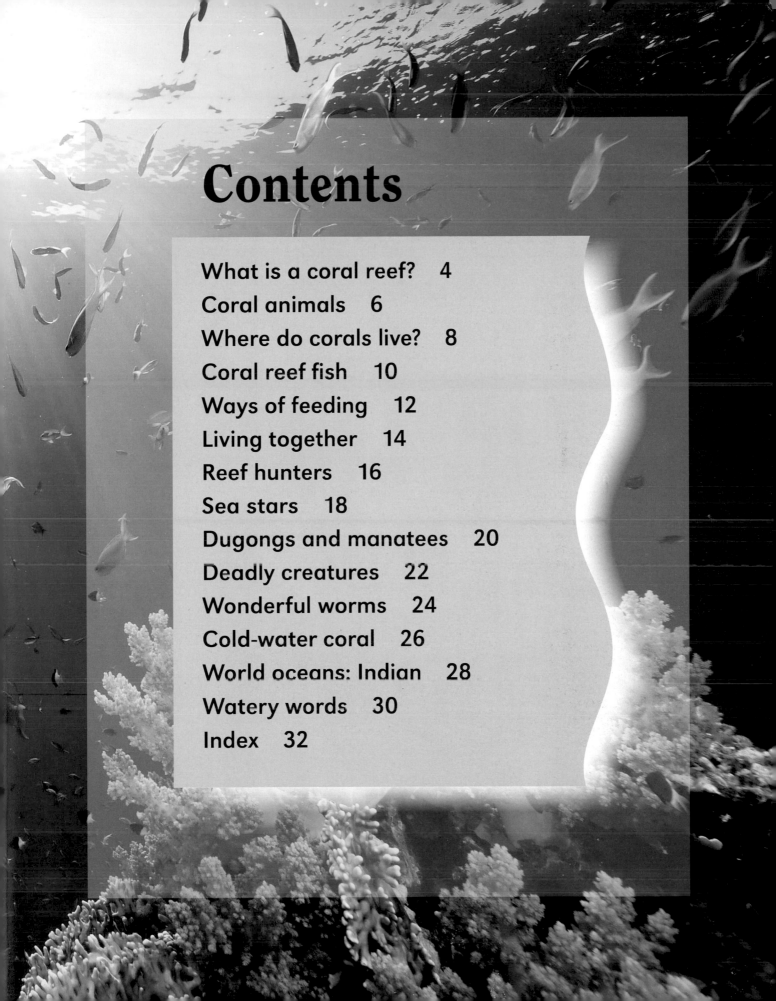

Contents

What is a coral reef?

Coral reefs are the busiest places in the oceans and lots of different kinds of animals live there. The reefs cover a tiny part (only one per cent) of the ocean floor, but they are home to a quarter of all sea creatures.

Guess what?

The Great Barrier Reef, off the coast of northeast Australia, is the biggest coral reef of all. It is more than 2,000 kilometres long – larger than the country of Italy.

Amazing!

Some of the world's coral reefs are more than 50 million years old.

A coral reef is made up of the **skeletons** of millions of coral animals, which look like little sea anemones. Each one has a rocky skeleton at its base. These coral skeletons build up on top of each other and form a huge reef. Many fish and other creatures come to the reef to feed on the coral and each other.

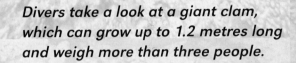

Divers take a look at a giant clam, which can grow up to 1.2 metres long and weigh more than three people.

Fish and lots of other animals live around coral reefs.

Coral animals

A single coral animal is called a **polyp**. Lots of polyps live close together in a group called a colony. Different kinds of coral make different shapes as the colony grows. Some are like mounds, while others look like the branches of a tree or large flat plates.

Some coral animals hatch from eggs and begin life floating in the ocean with other tiny creatures. Once the coral settles in one place, it makes lots of little copies of itself, each with its own hard base. During the day the coral polyps keep their **tentacles** tucked away, but at night they stretch them out to grab any passing food.

Lots of little coral polyps live in a brain coral colony. The shape of the colony is a bit like the surface of a human brain.

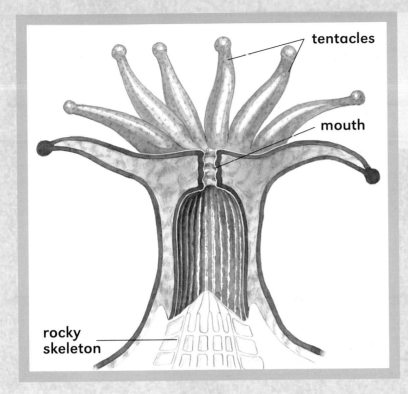

tentacles

mouth

rocky skeleton

A coral polyp has a rocky skeleton at its base. The polyp catches food with its tentacles and puts it in its mouth.

WATCH OUT!
Coral reefs are easily damaged and destroyed. Many experts think that three quarters of reefs will disappear over the next 30 or 40 years, unless we protect them better.

Amazing!

Coral reefs are the largest living structures **on our** planet.

A colony of staghorn coral makes branches which look like the antlers of a stag, or male deer.

Where do corals live?

Most coral reefs are in **tropical** areas near the **equator**, where the water is warm. Some reefs are close to the shore. These are called fringing reefs. Barrier reefs are a little further from land, while coral atolls are reefs around a sunken volcanic island.

Corals usually live in clear, shallow water. This is because tiny plants live inside the corals and, just like plants on land, these plants need sunlight to make food. The plants have a safe place to grow, while the corals get extra food. The plants also give the coral animals their colour.

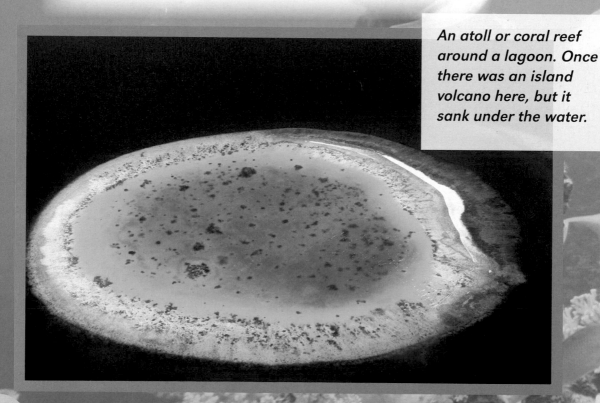

An atoll or coral reef around a lagoon. Once there was an island volcano here, but it sank under the water.

Not all corals contain tiny plants. This cup coral catches all its food with its long tentacles.

WATCH OUT!

Global warming can damage coral reefs. If the water gets warmer, the tiny plants may leave the coral. The coral will then lose its colour and it soon dies.

Some bleached coral on a reef.

Fringing and barrier reefs help to protect coasts from damage by storms and hurricanes.

Amazing!

Coral reef fish

Fish that live in the open sea have a **streamlined** shape which helps them cut quickly through the water. Coral reef fish look very different. They need to move around among the coral as they find food and avoid **predators**.

A queen angelfish nibbles sponges, sea fans and jellyfish. It has a speckled spot on its head which looks like a crown.

Amazing!

Young queen angelfish act as cleaners for other fish. They nibble little creatures called parasites which live on the skins of bigger fish.

Lots of coral reef fish have very flat bodies – they look like swimming discs. Their shape lets them twist and turn through the reef. They can also dive quickly into tiny gaps to avoid danger. Their fins help them steer.

Many coral fish are very brightly coloured. The patterns and colours may confuse predators, making the fish harder to see and catch.

This masked butterfly fish has a flat body.

Guess what?

The large dark eyespot on a butterfly fish may make a predator think that the little fish is bigger than it really is and keep it away.

This batfish is part of the spadefish family. The hazy bands across its flat body help it hide from predators.

Ways of feeding

There is lots of food for other animals in a coral reef. Reef fish have jaws and snouts which help them find and eat the food they like.

Parrotfish have very strong teeth that look like a beak. The fish uses them to scrape tiny plants called **algae** off the coral. It can even bite off lumps of hard coral skeleton. The moorish idol has a long snout it pokes into **crevices** to reach small **prey**. Triggerfish have such tough jaws and teeth they can even eat spiny sea urchins.

WATCH OUT!
People who have aquariums love beautiful coral reef fish. Many fish come from the sea and some, such as Banggai cardinalfish, are becoming rare. It is best to buy fish that have been specially bred.

A blue parrotfish. Can you see the beak-like teeth at the front of its mouth?

The spines of a triggerfish fold into a groove on its back when it doesn't need them.

Amazing!

A triggerfish has spines on its back. When it is threatened, it finds a hiding place and lifts its spines. The second spine locks the first one in place so the fish can't be moved.

The beautiful moorish idol fish has several long spines in its back fin that trail behind it as it swims.

Living together

A little boxer crab holds a sea anemone in each front claw and waves them to warn off enemies.

Some coral reef animals live with or on other animals which help them survive. The boxer crab scurries around the seabed with a small sea anemone on each front claw like a pair of pompoms.

The anemones can sting and the crab waves them at any predator that comes too near. The crab also gathers food with the sea anemones. The crab eats some of the food and the anemones have the rest.

Guess what?

The conical crab matches its colour to the coral it lives on. It sometimes breaks off bits of the coral and puts them on its own body to improve its disguise.

A sea cucumber crab sits on the back of a sea cucumber, grabbing any food that comes its way.

The sea cucumber crab lives on the body of a sea cucumber and feeds on the scraps from the cucumber's meals.

The little pearlfish goes one step further and spends its days inside the body of a sea cucumber. At night, it comes out to find small shrimp and other creatures to eat.

Pygmy sea horses are smaller than your little finger and live in coral. The sea horse is the same colour as the coral it lives on, so it is hard to spot.

Amazing!

15

Reef hunters

A barracuda has lots of teeth of different sizes. It sometimes chops prey into pieces before snapping it up.

Some fish come to the reef to hunt other fish, not to eat coral. One of the fiercest is the barracuda, a sharp-toothed fish that grows up to 1.8 metres long.

Barracuda usually hunt alone at night, but young barracuda sometimes swim and hunt in **schools**.

Groupers can be two metres long and they are good hunters. A grouper hides among coral until prey comes near,

Amazing!

The spines on the back of the lionfish are poisonous, but it uses them to defend itself, not to kill prey. The fish's bold stripes may warn off other fish!

Groupers drift slowly among the coral, but they can move very fast when chasing prey.

then opens its mouth wide to suck in the victim. Larger still are reef sharks and nurse sharks. They cruise the reef at night, eating anything they come across, from crabs to smaller sharks. The lionfish isn't a fast swimmer like barracuda and sharks, but lurks in wait for prey such as fish and shrimp.

Guess what?
When yellowmouth groupers hatch they are all female. Some turn into males once they are full grown.

The sharp spines on the back of a lionfish can give enemies a poisonous sting.

17

Sea stars

Lots of different kinds of starfish live on coral reefs, but the crown-of-thorns starfish is probably the greediest. It is about as big as a large dinner plate and glides over the reef munching lots of living coral.

Little brittle stars hide among coral and come out at night to feed. They eat **plankton** – tiny creatures drifting in the water – which they grab with long snakelike arms.

The crown-of-thorns turns the lining of its stomach out over the coral to digest it then pulls it all back in again.

Amazing!

Feather stars can crawl and swim with the help of their many arms.

Feather stars look more like branching plants than animals. A feather star has a cup-shaped body and 100 or more feathery arms. The arms have a sticky coating that help the starfish catch food.

Guess what?

Little harlequin shrimp feed on starfish. A male and female pair work together to turn the starfish over so it can't move. Then they eat up its little tube feet.

Dugongs and manatees

Dugongs and manatees are sometimes called sea cows. These gentle giants are related to elephants, but they spend all their lives in water. Like whales, they are **mammals**, not fish, and they come to the surface regularly to breathe air.

Many dugongs live around coral reefs. Some manatees live in rivers, but the West Indian manatee lives on coral reefs. This huge animal feeds on underwater grasses, which it finds with its bristly snout.

Dugongs are good divers and can stay under water for six minutes before coming up to take a breath.

A manatee has two long front flippers, each tipped with three or four nails.

Amazing!

Some people think that sailors who thought they had seen mermaids had really seen manatees.

WATCH OUT!

Manatees are becoming very rare. Many of these gentle, slow-moving animals are hurt when they collide with speedboats.

Manatees grow to about three metres long and weigh as much as six or seven people.

Deadly creatures

A few very dangerous animals live among the coral in some reefs. The box jellyfish has up to 60 long tentacles and each has 5,000 stinging cells. The jellyfish uses them to kill fish and shrimp. It is also very dangerous to humans.

The tentacles of the box jellyfish can be three metres long.

Amazing!

The poison of the box jellyfish is very strong, but sea turtles can eat them without being harmed.

The banded sea snake has a flat tail shaped like a paddle to help it swim.

Sea snakes have a very poisonous bite too. The poison lets the snake **paralyse** its prey before it has a chance to swim away.

Another deadly hunter is the little blue-ringed octopus. This creature is only about 20 cm long and has a head the size of the golf ball, but it is one of the most poisonous creatures in the world. It paralyses prey with its bite, which doesn't hurt, but can kill even humans.

Guess what?

Most of the time the blue-ringed octopus is grey or brown, but when it is scared blue rings appear on its body. The rings are a warning that it is about to attack.

Wonderful worms

The worms that live on coral reefs are very different from the wiggly brown creatures in our gardens. Most amazing is the Christmas tree worm, which has two spirals of tentacles shaped like little Christmas trees.

The worm lives in a tube it makes in coral and sticks out its tentacles to grab tiny animals and other food from the water.

A Christmas tree worm can fold up its tentacles and disappear into its burrow.

Amazing!

The Christmas tree worm uses its feathery tentacles for breathing as well as for feeding. These worms can be different colours, such as blue, white, yellow and orange.

The colourful fireworm feeds on coral as it moves around the reef. It has rows of stinging bristles along each side.

The feather duster worm also lives in a tube either in a reef or on the seabed. Its head has a fan of feathery tentacles that catch food.

An orange fireworm. Look out for its stinging bristles.

The feather duster worm's tentacles can be 10 centimetres across.

WATCH OUT!
Coral reefs and their wildlife are beautiful, but they are also useful to millions of people who live near them and gather food from them. We need to make sure that the reefs are kept safe today and in the future.

Cold-water coral

People used to think that corals only lived in warm water in tropical parts of the world, but scientists have found types of coral that live in cold, deep water.

There are more than 4,000 kinds of cold-water coral. These coral animals do not have tiny plants living inside them, unlike the coral that lives in warm water. Cold-water corals feed on tiny creatures floating by which they catch with sticky tentacles. Their reefs are home to lots of worms, shellfish and other creatures.

Cold-water corals in the Atlantic Ocean, off the coast of Norway.

WATCH OUT!
Cold-water corals are very delicate and easily damaged by **pollution** and fishing nets. The reefs grow very slowly and it takes hundreds of years to repair damage.

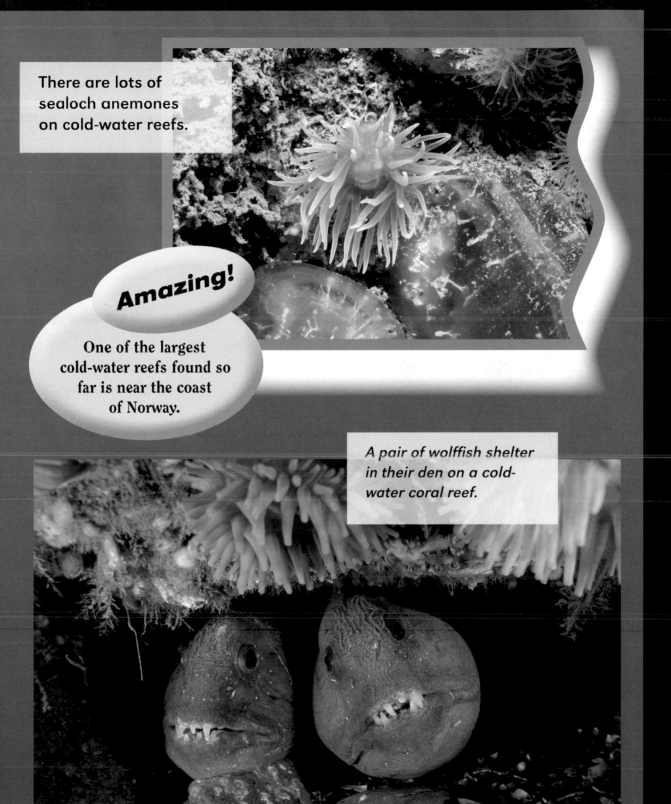

There are lots of sealoch anemones on cold-water reefs.

Amazing!

One of the largest cold-water reefs found so far is near the coast of Norway.

A pair of wolffish shelter in their den on a cold-water coral reef.

27

World oceans: Indian

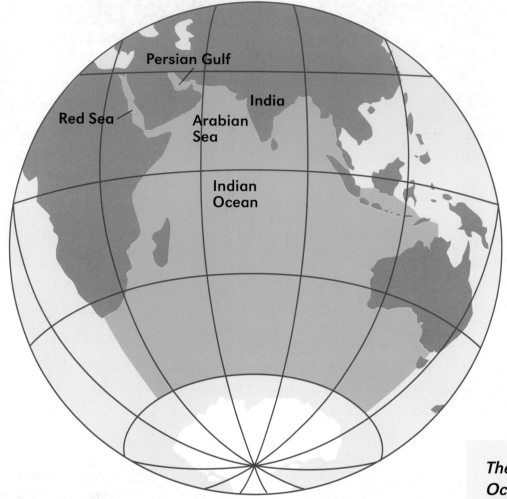

Persian Gulf

India

Red Sea

Arabian Sea

Indian Ocean

The Indian Ocean is the third largest ocean in the world. It lies between Africa, Asia and Australia and is north of the Southern Ocean. The Indian Ocean includes the Red Sea, the Arabian Sea and the Persian Gulf. In 2004 a huge earthquake in the Indian Ocean set off a series of **tsunamis** or tidal waves. These killed thousands of people and caused damage in many countries around the Indian Ocean.

The Indian Ocean is the only ocean that is named after a country – India.

Indian Ocean facts

The Indian Ocean covers about 68,550 square kilometres. That is more than five times the size of the United States.

The deepest point of the Indian Ocean is the Java trench, which is 7,258 metres deep. The highest mountain in North America, Mount McKinley, would disappear in this trench.

The Indian Ocean is nearly 10,000 kilometres across between southern Africa and Australia, where it is widest.

The many islands in the Indian Ocean include the Andaman Islands, Sri Lanka, Madagascar, Mauritius and the Maldives.

Rivers that flow into the Indian Ocean include the Zambesi, the Indus and the Ganges.

Zheng He was a Chinese sailor and explorer. In the 15th century he led amazing voyages from China across the Indian Ocean to Africa.

Watery words

algae
Plants that live in water. Most algae do not have true leaves or roots.

crevice
A narrow opening or crack.

equator
An imaginary line round the middle of the Earth.

global warming
A rise in the temperature of the world that some experts think is caused by human activities.

hurricane
A very powerful storm with strong winds and heavy rain.

mammal
A warm-blooded animal that feeds its babies with milk from its own body.

paralyse
To make another animal unable to move.

plankton
Tiny plants and animals that live floating in the water. Most cannot be seen with the naked eye.

pollution
The introduction of things that damage the natural world, such as litter and oil.

polyp
A small animal with a soft body.

predator
An animal that hunts and kills other animals to eat.

prey
An animal that is hunted and eaten by another animal.

school (of fish)
A group of fish that swim together.

skeleton
The hard part of an animal's body that supports the softer parts.

streamline
To make a neat shape that moves easily through water.

structure
A structure is something that has been built.

tentacles
Long parts of an animal's body, used for feeling and holding food.

tropical
A tropical place has a very hot, wet climate. Areas around the equator are tropical.

tsunami
An extremely large and powerful sea wave, caused by an earthquake or a volcanic eruption.

Index